# Bipolar Express

Gabriel Cougar Burt

ISBN: **1511866837**
ISBN-13: **978-1511866835**

# DEDICATION

Thank you to everyone who was there for me when I needed help the

most

# PLAYLIST

# PROLOGUE

I was thirty-one years old when I lost my mind. I had alienated a
lot of my friends, quit my job without any notice, and moved
across the country. It took a long time to hit rock bottom but when
I did, my only hope was that I would survive, one day thrive, and
help others learn from my mistakes.

# 1 FATHER AND SON

How can I try to explain, when I do he turns away again

Its always been the same, same old story

From the moment I could talk I was ordered to listen

Now there's a way and I know that I have to go away.

I know I have to go.

*-Cat Stevens*

I was born a baby. A fat, angry baby. I would cry as soon as I woke up if my food wasn't ready. I feel like I'm to blame for my parents not having more children. Luckily, I mellowed out once I figured out where my parents hid the Doritos.

Luckily, at the age of five I got a serious case of pneumonia and lost a lot of weight. It was hell on my lungs but

1

great for my core. I don't like to brag but all the girls tried to sleep next to me at naptime. I was kind of a big deal.

I was raised in a fairly strict Christian home in a small Texas town called Merkel that boasted of nothing more than the kindest people I've ever met. It has no stoplights and most of its four way stops work on the honor system. If it wasn't for the rampant meth production and lack of trees, it could be a decent town.

The Windmill City, as no one actually calls it, will always be where I consider home. My family has always moved like a pack of gypsies that was wanted for killing a foreign dignitary. I went to four different schools growing up and was also homeschooled for a bit. I feel like I came out fairly normal considering I was homeschooled for any amount of time. My parents also almost named me Jedediah so I'm not unaccustomed to dodging bullets.

We lived in Merkel longer than anywhere else. It's where I started school and where I made most of my lifelong friends.

When I think of my childhood I think of Merkel. I think of the nights that I felt so alive and so in tune with my group of friends. That's something I very rarely feel these days.

A plus of growing up in a small Texas town is that, even all these years later, I could call any of my old friends and I have no doubt they would help me if I needed it. My very first best friend was a beautiful blond girl named Janae who, unfortunately for me, grew into a beautiful woman that I've willingly been in the friend zone with for twenty-nine years and counting.

Both of my parents were raised in ultra conservative homes so I really lucked out that I wasn't spanked more. Both of my grandfathers were preachers at different times in their lives. This fact definitely affected the way I was raised and also the way I view organized religion. It's hard to have a real favorable view of organized religion when you see your grandparents have to move because they angered the wrong person in their congregation.

My father, Dennis, was a field goal kicker in high school and tried out for the Dallas Cowboys at one point. He has worked for the phone company ever since he graduated from high school save for an indeterminate period of time where he lived in his van down by the river. True story.

My mother, Lesa, is the sweetest spitfire you will ever meet. She's one of the strongest people I know. She went back to school at the age of fifty to become a nurse. She hated it but that's a different story. My brother, Jeremy, was the best brother I could even think to ask for. He played football in high school which means a lot in Texas. I've looked up to him from that point on.

I started school a year late because I was a little small for my age. On top of that, I had a really bad speech impediment that made it about impossible to understand me. If it wasn't for that bout with pneumonia I may have ended up sleeping in the corner. Just me and the smelly kid. There's always one.

I stayed at Merkel with the majority of my present core of friends til fourth grade when we all got drafted to go fight Saddam. Kidding. My family moved into Abilene to our school's rival, Wylie. It's funny, looking back, how serious this move seemed at the time. The entire town was upset with my parents for moving my brother out of their football program. You would have thought my parents moved Jason Street out of Dillon, you know, before his accident. Texas football, yall.

At Wylie I learned that I was weird. It really helped prepare me for the twenty-one years that have followed. In my bullies' defense, I am weird. I've always seen the world differently than most everyone. Even still, I made a lot of great friends at Wylie but I'm sad to say that things really slowed down in the lady department. I told myself it was more about quality than quantity but we all know the truth: knowing your multiplication facts wasn't cool anymore.

I would still go back and visit Merkel randomly but it was really weird missing out on so much of people's lives that you care about. This was back when it was actually hard to stay in contact with people. Can you remember that? We were literally only thirty or so miles away but I might as well have been in the French Foreign Legion.

This was back when calls thirty minutes away were long distance and cost at least a dime a minute. How often do you think I was able to convince my parents to make those calls? My only other plan was to buy a lot of string and a couple of cans to build a very intricate phone system. Unfortunately, that plan came to a drastic halt as the string ran out midway down our driveway.

In seventh grade, we made an actually big move to Colorado. Estes Park, to be exact. It's a beautiful area but, even from the beginning, Colorado and I have not gotten along. Sure, it was nice when we would go visit when I was younger but that all went out the window when we actually made a commitment and moved there. On our very first day I got lost in the national forest and was chased by an elk. You read that right.

What had happened was we were unpacking the truck and decided to take a break and drive the good old Subaru up to the national forest. While we were walking around my brother broke off on his own and after, I'm assuming, a lot of griping on my part I got the feeling that I wouldn't be missed if I gave my parents some free time. It took about five seconds for me to get lost. It took about five more seconds for me to go into survival mode.

We had read Hatchet that year in school so I felt abnormally, although incorrectly, prepared for life in the wild. I can still remember walking close to the ground in a very stealth like manner that probably wasn't all that stealthy. Thirty minutes or so later I ran up on what ended up not being a wild mustang sent to me by God. Long story short, I apparently had stumbled upon a mother elk and her baby. I did my best to channel Emmitt Smith and bolted out of there. My assumptions that I was just too fast for the elk may be erroneous. Either way, I'm alive to tell the tale.

In addition to angry woodland creatures, Colorado introduced me to the majesty of scrambled late night Cinemax. My eyes were wide open, ya know, until I had to squint to make sure I was seeing things clearly. It was soon after that I got caught in Hastings using a copy of "The Old Man and the Sea" to hide a playboy that was a good three inches wider than the literary classic.

I had gotten very introverted in Colorado. I barely wanted

to leave the house and that wasn't only because of the scrambled pornography. I felt totally alone and separated from those around me. This was the first time in my life I remember feeling so disconnected. Unfortunately, this is a feeling that I live with daily now. It may just be a part of growing up but it sucks.

This feeling of listlessness and loneliness has always driven me in so many ways. It drove me to be funny so people would like me. It drove me through college when I was told and believed that a college degree would fix everything. Who knows, maybe it will when I'm done paying it off.

A few months later we ended up back in Merkel for the majority of my seventh and eighth grade years. To date, this was my longest, happiest time in my life. I met two of my best friends, rekindled other friendships, and –most importantly- I discovered sarcasm. It was a big time for me. At the end of my eighth grade year my family moved to Colorado Springs, Colorado and I never lived in Merkel again.

I had no signs of mental health issues at this age. There

have been instances in my family before but I clearly hoped that it would skip over me. The only telltale sign was my inherant rage, as a baby, when I woke and my meal wasn't already prepared to my liking. I would scream bloody murder until I was pleased, much like Joffrey in Game of Thrones. I would not make a good king. I also had a flair for the theatrics as I would grow angry and stomp my way up the stairs only to instantly turn around at the top of the stairs and be cool.

When I was younger I blamed my parents for these moves but that's not fair. They did their best with the cards they were dealt and I hold no ill will towards anyone. That being said, all the moves (there are more than I mentioned) made it way too easy to leave people. I never knew until this last move just how self destructive moving is. I have moved myself far more than my parents ever dreamed of moving me. I move because I'm always looking for that one thing that will fill that void under my ribs that yearns for something real. I'm just now realizing that void is me and its not gonna go away until I figure out myself and what my purpose is.

High School was a difficult time for me. My first day of high school was at a new school in Colorado Springs that had drastically new expectations of me. Colorado Springs is a great place full of great people, but for me, it always just reminded me of the ice planet Hoth in Empire. I spent the majority of my time thinking about my friends in Texas which, I see now, really kept me from enjoying Colorado more than I did.

To say that the educational system in Merkel was a little bit behind would have been a drastic understatement. I basically skated through school and life through eighth grade. I can even remember convincing my eighth grade science teacher that, due to my religious beliefs I didn't feel comfortable judging others and I was forced to choose true on every true/false question. I'd like to thank Zack Morris for me having no idea how the world works both scientifically and socially. Time outs, sadly, don't work in real life.

When we moved to Colorado, I was enrolled in a private Christian school called Colorado Springs Christian School. CSCS, to me, was harder than college ever was but, of course, I did get a

General Studies degree. The one saving point of Colorado was the people I met there. I made some amazing friends that I still have today. One of which was my locker partner who was awesome enough to let me stay at his place years later when I just happened to be in Newport, California. Twice.

Looking back I'm really surprised anyone liked me because I was so unhappy and spent most of my time talking about Texas and the people I knew there. I was probably lucky that I met them in high school, the one time and place you can be a melancholic, sarcastic tool and excel at making friends.

The one thing I did not excel at was my school work. I had never had to work for my grades and I definitely had no plans of starting. I was too busy trying to memorize the choreography of the dance scene at the beginning of the original Austin Powers movie. I may still remember those dance moves but I'll never admit to it.

My lack of dedication to my studies was made even more apparent when one of my best friends, Joel, visited from Texas and went to school with me. It was a little awkward getting sent out to the hall when you have a guest with you. Sending someone out to the hall to mingle with the passersby is not a good way to punish children. Some of my fondest memories of high school happened while all the chumps were grading their work. Granted a large majority of those chumps have Masters Degrees now but they did miss out on that time the hot, hot, blonde senior whose locker was right next to Mrs. Vidlak's room actually talked to us. If Facebook had existed back then, mine woulda blown up.

High school was the first time I had trouble with depression. I'm not sure if, at this point, it was situational because I wanted to be in Texas or if it was the first signs of being bipolar. I don't really remember if I had mood swings back then or not. All I do remember is how amazing I got at biting sarcasm in high school. I could burn someone with the greatest of ease.

I, with the usual couth of a teenager, definitely didn't hold back on teachers either. One poor, good-hearted freshman science teacher got the majority of my "charm". In retrospect, being a Science teacher at a staunchly Christian school really should've been trying enough for her. She didn't need my help to question her choices in life. To her credit, she only gave me detention once and that was for not having my book covered. It took me about two years to realize how awful I had been. I called her back years later to apologize for my behavior.

Before I come off like a saint for that, I never called and apologized to the hump-backed teacher I asked about the difficulty of her commute to work from her bell tower because she wouldn't let me use my birthday coupon. I can still remember the shock in everyone's eyes when I asked. Two were very attractive girls and the other was a freshman that I just called "prick" when I needed him. Boy, I was a real treat. He also never received an apologetic phone call. And we all know at some point he will end up being my boss because that's how life works.

I've basically worked since the summer before seventh grade and that continued through high school. I have easily had over thirty different jobs. I can't tell you how many times I 'no call no showed' as a teenager and into my twenties. I always half expected to see myself on the side of a milk carton.

For the majority of high school I worked at my parents'
popcorn store which was exhausting. I hate popcorn now. I can
barely stomach the smell. Pikes Peak Gourmet Popcorn was the
name and Im sure they're still open if you want some chocolate
covered popcorn. I know I've done a great job of selling the
product. It kind of ruins it when you have to stay up all night
cooking it. One good thing about the popcorn store was I met a
very special girl there. She liked the way I pronounced cherry
(cheery) so I bought her a snow globe and a CD with her favorite
song, Strawberry Wine, on it.

The popcorn store was one of the first places, looking
back, I can see some of my troubles with bipolar swings showing
up. I've never self-medicated with illegal drugs but I was lucky
enough to live in the age when actual ephedrine was legal and in
Advocare Sparks. I would have at least three or four a day and
work like crazy. From what I've read, bipolars tend to work on a
25 hour a day clock meaning that we're always trying to get that
extra hour at the expense of sleep or quality life choices. I can't
tell you how many times I worked all day, all night, and a little bit

of the next day. My longest shift was about twenty seven hours and, because I worked for my parents, it wasn't discouraged.

Unfortunately, I met Snow Globe at a very tumultuous time in my life. I had been on Wellbutrin for a while and I actually needed it. It was about midway through my sophomore year and my lack of interest in school was starting to come to fruition. My only saving grace was that my hardest class, which actually interested me, also had my highest grade. Israeli Language and Culture probably sounds boring but it was just 'off the wall' enough to hold my interest. Also, the teacher, Mr. Gordon, didn't talk down to us and I enjoyed that.

I struggled through all of my other classes for about a month and then on Valentine's Day of sophomore year I withdrew from school. I would like to say that all the girls were devastated and refused to celebrate the holiday that year but it would be a lie.

Looking back, I think both of my parents would agree that this was a huge mistake that set in motion a general disregard to logic and the value of just "going with the flow" of society.

There's a reason the majority of people do something like finish high school in four year instead of by passing a single test.

I feel like I really missed out on a lot of social growth that has just made me more weird or out of step with everyone else. I missed out on so many fun times I could have had with my friends and so much possibility of personal growth. I think if someone, like me, tends to be a little weird anyway, having them finish high school alone at the kitchen table may not be the best move.

That's what happened though. I studied for my GED and passed without any trouble. At the ripe old age of sixteen, I began taking college classes. A short seven years later I still hadn't graduated with a doctorate in procrastination but I was gonna get to it. Tomorrow. I did really well the first semester because it was new and challenging. I came out of the first semester with three A's and one B which was great. The problem came the next semester when the whole college thing seemed old hat already.

I ended up dropping most of my classes that semester. The majority of the problem came from a Statistics class that I wasn't prepared for with my two and a half years of missing Math and an English class which was led by a brazenly, openly homosexual man. Coming straight (no pun intended) out of Christian school to a teacher that made us read all anti Church propaganda was a little unsettling to say the least. This was back around 2000 when there was very little tolerance, if any, between homosexuals and Christians.

I wish I knew what I know now and I probably could have seen a lot more value in his point of view. I can't imagine how it must have felt, or how it feels for that matter, to get that much heat from the outside world over such a personal choice.

This was around the time I had my first panic attack. From what I understand now, Welbutrin can actually make anxiety worse. I remember it was a cold summer day and all I could do was sit in my room and cry/freak out. I, of course, told no one. Why would I? Oh yeah, to get help. It was around this time that I tried to reconnect with that special girl from the popcorn store and I was already a mess.

It didn't work out, in the end, because we were seventeen. I value those times looking back. This was the first time in my life I felt so anxious that I couldn't stay seated most of the time. I still remember that I left "The New Guy" with DJ Qualls about halfway through because I just couldn't sit still anymore. In the theater or in life. So I drove home, packed up some stuff, and basically just struck out on my own. Looking back, I was extremely manic.

# 2 KING OF THE ROAD

I ain't got no cigarettes

Ah, but, two hours of pushin' broom

Buys an eight by twelve four-bit room

I'm a man of means by no means

King of the road.

*-Roger Miller*

Being in control of your own life is a freedom you think, as a child, is the apex of living. I used that freedom to drive down every highway I could find. In retrospect, I probably needed a conservatorship as much as Britney Spears and Lindsey Lohan ever did. I was listless and had nothing anchoring me down. It's honestly hard to even remember half of the things that I've done.

For almost half of my life, I have been my own worst enemy. I love the person that I am, to a degree. The problem is that person can become manic and the parts that I love become so magnified that they're no longer healthy or logical. I'm a light hearted person that will do anything for anyone.

Within reason, there's nothing wrong with that. Unfortunately, I rarely live in logical parameters. I'd like to blame movies for expecting too much of myself but a lot of it is my disorder. I push myself harder than I should and think I should be able to do things no other person could or would do. I have asked myself to do things that were as selfless as they were self-destructive.

That may be one drawback of growing up in church like I did. I was always taught to take care of and love others but no one ever said anything about loving yourself. You should do for others but you should also make sure you're in good shape yourself. God loves me as much as my neighbor and I need to take equal care of both.

The biggest case and point I can think of is when I couldn't have been older than ten because I was reading a cheat book for NBA Jam Tournament Edition at the time. I was sitting there figuring out how to get one of the Beastie Boys on my team and for some reason I started thinking about the rapture and tribulation. Yeah, weird kid.

I started to think about all of the people that would be here lost without any help and I decided I should really be here to help but realized I couldn't be because I'd be raptured. In hopes of being able to help, I remembered that in the Bible it said that if you cursed the Holy Spirit you wouldn't be forgiven so I did.

I used whatever I thought was a curse word at the time and felt pleased with myself that I was going to be able to help all those people. I was gonna have to go through hell on Earth but I'd be able to help people. That decision haunted me for years when I realized the severity of that decision until I ultimately realized I had misunderstood the scripture but that's where my head is at on helping people. Its not healthy.

I'm very adventurous and think outside the box which is probably why I was willing to put myself through seven years of hell. But I think that's a reason I make friends so easily. That and all the moving made me really good at meeting people. However, it did not give me many skills for maintaining friendships.

A lot of my abilities come from a manic place. I hate being the new person in a room or group. It's a total fight or flight scenario for me. What most people see as witty anecdotes or original sarcastic one liners are usually just blind luck or lifted from old Fresh Prince episodes. I can still quote most every episode word for word and haven't watched one in years. I may seem chill in those situations but in my head I'm sporadic and flailing about trying to find something funny to say.

The first thing I did when I got back to Texas, being free of my parents for the first time in my life, was go to my friend Joel's house where we laid by the pool for a few days. I had money saved up and I decided to live off that for awhile so I could reset my mind and figure out my next few steps.

My mom called my favorite aunt and asked if I could stay with her while I figured out everything. I love this aunt deeply and took the offer immediately. It didn't hurt that my younger cousins had an extremely hot babysitter named Taryn.

I still remember sitting with my aunt and uncle looking at the college catalog for the local community college and flipping through the pages trying to figure out what I wanted to be. I would flip through a few pages and then randomly point out a subject and see if that was what I wanted to be. I'm sure it was in no way damaging for my impressionable cousins to see me make an important decision in such a way.

I ultimately decided on nursing because I thought it would be easy to find a job. The only problem was that I hated sick people and had the worst gag reflex in the world. I couldn't even be in the same room as black-eyed peas, the food and band alike, without gagging. I tried to put this aside and just make things work even though I knew it was going to be an uphill battle.

I was a nursing major for about a month. What killed that dream was a science professor that wanted us to actually learn something and that was not the reason I attended class every day. My perfect attendance was more based on the super-hot brunette that sat in the lobby randomly. Her name was Shea and I had a huge crush on her when we both went to school at Wylie. She, on the other hand, had no idea who I was. A few days of casual stalking later, I got the guts to go up and talk to her.

It's important to note that, at this time, I was overweight and let my rebellion against my parents be known by my ever growing hair that was at my shoulders around this time. To this day, I'm thankful that Shea didn't mace the Chris Farley look-a-like that pulled a chair up next to her. I may have skipped my music appreciation class to sit and talk which I think we can all agree was wise. I'm never gonna need anything they taught in that class. A few months and a haircut later, Shea actually told me where she lived and we've been best friends ever since.

I had as many majors in college as I did actual colleges I attended. I went to South Plains (technically), Cisco Junior

College two times, University of Texas in Arlington twice, and Texas Tech twice. I have so many wasted hours of college credit. The technical attendance at South Plains consisted of me going for two hours of an eight hour orientation. I left when I saw how tiny my dorm room was and how large my roommate was. The room was so small that I would have had to move my bed each time I wanted to close the door.

My list of majors includes nursing, political science, film, electronic communications, and ultimately General Studies so that I could use my wasted hours for something worthwhile. Unfortunately, there wasn't a General Studies factory anywhere near me so it didn't do a lot of good. I remember thinking, though, that I could not go to college longer than Tommy Callahan and it ended up being really close.

I continued to have a lot of different jobs because nothing could hold my interest and people rarely questioned me about it. My parents were laid back in that aspect of my life and that's something I won't be able to do knowing what I know about myself. I make the world's worst decisions. Where most people weigh options and rule out bad decisions I think "Oh yeah, Indiana Jones would totally go to Tunisia right now". I can't tell you how many times not having a passport saved me. I honestly spend way too much time thinking 'what would some movie or TV character do' in this situation. The difference being the repercussions for their actions only last thirty minutes or so.

I've really only been able to have two relationships of any respectful length; one of which was an English major, named Jessica. It was nice to have someone around that understood my need to write and get thoughts out of my head. I think the reason I wasn't able to hold on to any relationships is the anxiety and stress I had in my life from being bipolar. It's really hard to know how you feel about someone when you don't really know how you feel about yourself.

My living situation was no less messy. I was originally supposed to stay with my aunt but a night spent in their house alone combined with the poor choice of watching "The Devil's Advocate" scared me so much that I've only slept there three times since and always with others there. I'm usually that guy that answers your craigslist ad and sleeps on a couch or a pile of towels on the floor. For real. I've grown very accustomed to living with strangers.

I wish I would have realized back then that there is a reason people do things a certain way. If you can't tell that's a recurring theme. For me, the questions should go: if no one else is jumping off the cliff, maybe you shouldn't either.

# 3 I WOKE UP IN A CAR

I woke up in a car ,I traced away the fog

so I could see the Mississippi on her knees

I've never been so lost I've never felt so much at home

please write my folks and throw away my keys

*-Something Corporate*

There are a lot of suspect decisions that I've made through the years.  Among the worst was during my spring semester of my freshman year.  As I've said, I moved to Texas against the wishes of my parents.  I had spent the summer and fall hanging out and staying with my friend and his family.  This was all, of course, after Al Pacino and an exceptionally windy night ruined my aunt's house for me.

Much like the story of the Ant and the Grasshopper, winter came. It came a lot faster than in Game of Thrones. We're all waiting R.R.! I had taken classes in the fall and I was working for free movies at my friend's family's video store. It was also all the free coke and candy you could eat as long as you didn't get caught.

I stayed at my grandmother's some to placate my parents a little bit. Unfortunately, around the end of December my grandmother to decided to move forty five minutes away so I had to figure out a place to stay. I knew I was welcome at my friend's house but I hated to need to stay with someone.

My mom, who was supportive even if she disagreed with my actions called and asked Janae's parents if I could stay with them. They, of course, said yes. I don't really remember talking to my dad as much as this point in my life. I think I was angry with my parents in general for all the moves but there's no way to stay mad at your mom. Even Eminem couldn't do it!

The problem still was that I didn't want to be a bother to anyone. That's when I got the bright idea to live in my three-door

Saturn coupe. Now, I know what you're thinking but I took care of that problem by parking at the local truck stop. What I would do is basically go back and forth between my two friends' houses and also my grandmother's in Sweetwater. It was your classic Brady Bunch scheme.

The only time I could be found for sure at one of the three places was when I needed a shower. I may have been too prideful to let my true neediness known but I was nowhere near being okay with showering with truckers. We all remember what almost happened to Lloyd Christmas.

There are a lot of plusses about living in your car. One, the commute to and from work is great. I thought about getting a roommate so I could use the HOV lanes. Also, there's no wondering where you put something. Whatever you were looking for was right under your head and it was sharp. Finally, it's a lot easier to take a girl home when you live in your car. After they find that out, though, things get a little bit tougher.

The whole time I was doing this I was also taking four or

five classes at Cisco Junior College. I think they were all night classes so I literally just sat in my car most of the day. My grades were still decent but that said more about the weaknesses of CJC than my abilities as a student.

I would just tool around all day, go by one of my friend's house, get a shower, and play some video games. After telling them I had stayed at one of the other people's house I would grab some food and sit and talk for a bit. If it got super cold, as it can randomly in Texas, I would show up at one of the other two places and say something about getting locked out and not wanting to bother anyone. I knew I was being stupid but it was fun and exciting after being stuck in Colorado.

Don't forget that this was also when I had the wild idea to have long hair. Because, I guess, I didn't look homeless enough. This was before Tim Riggins but I'd like to think they based his character off my rugged look at the time. Did I ever play Texas high school football? No, but I did wear a lot of athletics sweats so we were pretty similar.

I had a nice little living situation going in my car. The passenger seat was my home office, the back seat was where I entertained. The trunk is where I kept all my clothes and belongings. It is also where I slept. A pile of hoodies is actually pretty comfortable. I would use the driver's seat for driving and personal grooming. I dried my hair many times by speeding through the country with the window rolled down and my head sticking out Scooby Doo style.

One time I was going out to the lake one night because I thought it would be cool to sleep out there. I parked and a few minutes later this creepy van pulled up and it was….well, creepy. It looked like they were trying to dump a body so I left rather quickly. About a month later, I found out on the news that about a month earlier a body was dumped right where I was. Thank you, God, for saving me.

It's really not that hard to fall asleep in a car. I would just park somewhere, like the truck stop under a streetlight, crawl into the den (the backseat), pop the seat down and crawl into the trunk and sleep on my clothes. If I got self conscious I would just cover my head up with a T-shirt.

I think its important to point out  that I was not on drugs or even drinking at the time.

I was just naturally stupid.  In retrospect, I was manic.  I wasn't on drugs, technically, but the feelings of mania unknowingly had me high as a kite.  I didn't realize it, until recently, that I would consume insane levels of caffeine (through Advocare Sparks and caffeine pills at the time) to keep me at manic levels as much as possible.

Funny side story about caffeine pills and this time in my life.  I guess it was 2003 and Valentine's Day was coming up. Shockingly, I was single.  I'll give you a second to process that. Well, I got the bright idea that I should try and sleep all the way through Valentine's Day.  Yes.  Was this logical? No, but what would be the most logical way to make this happen?  Sleeping pills the day of, right?  Wrongo, friend.

Starting February 12th, I started pumping my body full of caffeine, sparks, and whatever caffeine pill was popular at the time. I stayed up for forty-eight hours straight and showed up at my grandmother's. I doubt that I looked well. On the way there, I went and got a movie to watch to make me pass out even harder.

This is where it took a dark turn. To anyone that doesn't know, "The Last Picture Show" may be the most depressing movie ever made. I laid down at 1130 that night after not sleeping for forty-eight or so hours and put it in, on VHS mind you. At midnight, I was still wide awake. At one, I was still awake. This went on all night. Finally around six in the morning I passed out. Sadly at this very point my grandmother was waking up to take the dog out and you better believe when I heard the door I sprung into action much like a younger Chuck Norris and slammed the door shut on the intruder. All at once, I saved my grandmother's life and bruised the entire left side of her body. That's love.

I'm pretty sure this was also the year that I got a concussion from riding a shopping cart up the steepest jump at the skating park. Don't worry, I didn't wear a helmet. I only remember three things about that event. One, I really should've accepted the helmet offered to me seconds before. Two, I really don't like the friend that pushed me. Three, my tongue was really numb afterwards.

# 4 GRADUATE

Can I graduate?

Can I look at faces that I meet?

Can I get my punk ass off the street?

I've been living on for so long.

-Third Eye Blind

Somehow amidst all these bad decisions and moves I found a way to graduate from college. This came after finally realizing I needed to buckle down and do something with my life. Unfortunately, that meant me buckling down to get a General Studies degree which has done very little to help my standing in the world.

I showed up late to my graduation and in shorts and sandals. Don't worry, they were leather. The real problem with choosing to wear shorts to graduation was that it made it look like I was naked under my gown. When they told us to turn off our cell phones I got mine out and called my grandmother that couldn't make it to graduation. I spent the majority of graduation texting people because it was so, so boring.

Reality hits college graduates really hard after graduation. This was especially true for me. A few weeks after I graduated from college my parents got divorced. I remember it vividly because my dad left as I was on the way to WalMart and can still remember actually thinking that things were going really well and that I was truly happy. Then I got home.

My parents were married for thirty-one years and that's a lot longer than most. They did their best. The longest relationship I've had was with a tootsie-pop trying to disprove Mr. Owls answer of three.

When I pulled back up from WalMart I was still the guy

that could drop everything and leave at a moment's notice and believed everything always worked out for the best. When I got in the house that all changed. There are few things as devastating as watching your mom or dad in pain so coming home to both of them that way rocked me.

When I graduated with my General Studies degree, my plan was to use it to be able to go overseas and teach English. That all changed when I got back home. My dad was going to Colorado and my Mom was going to stay in Texas. There was absolutely no way that I would leave my mom at this point in her life. It was at this point that I changed. I knew I couldn't be a kid anymore and that I had to grow up. The only good aspect of it was that I desperately needed to grow up and this forced me into it.

The biggest change for me was that my general outlook in life changed drastically. I went from thinking that things will work out and that I had some magical journey ahead of me to just being a down to earth in the dirt angry person. That's what will happen when the rug gets pulled out from underneath you. I had never really been an angry person before but from the moment I walked in that door til I hit rock bottom (a little over five years) I was governed and driven by rage.

There are some upsides to being driven by rage. You get a lot done. You usually lose weight because you're too mad to eat and you're so mad that you work out like crazy. I lost about thirty pounds from pushing myself as hard as I could. I didn't know it at the time but pushing myself so hard and not feeding my body pushed me into a manic state and I became addicted to that feeling.

Mania honestly feels great. The only problem is that it is in no way sustainable.

Before my parent's divorce, I mainly listened to indie rock and fairly happy music but ever since I more often than not listen to rap because it's usually angry. My favorite rappers are Jay Z, Kanye, and Eminem.

I know realistically I was nowhere near their level of being 'hard' on the outside but my inner monologue steadily became that of Eminem. I talked to myself and was as hard on myself as I thought he would be. I honestly hated myself and any remnant of the person I used to be pissed me off. What I was summed up to the status quo that got me to the place I was so I set out to change almost everything about myself and make myself a harder person. I did this because I never wanted to be the victim of anything ever again. I set out to be the best man I could be. And not in a boy scout kind of way. Much like Warren G, I wanted it all.

Basically, the person I was no longer made sense to me in the world that I found myself in. Not wanting to leave the country while my family was in shambles, I got my emergency certification for teaching but while I did this I had to work at a local grocery store. My coworkers were great but there's something that dies inside when you work for a little over minimum wage and have a bachelor's degree you have to pay for.

At no point has my mom ever asked me to stay nearby or do anything that wasn't in my own interests. She always wanted me to live my own life and not worry about her. I'm just not good at that. I struggle with faith that prayer is enough. There are countless times that I've gone above and beyond for someone simply because prayer doesn't sound like enough to me. Sure, I do pray about it but then in the back of my head I try to think of a practical way to help on my own.

When you hate the world that you're living in, it doesn't take long for you to also hate yourself. I know I said this before but I didn't realize how bad it was until I hit rock bottom. I was awful to everyone. I gave no one any slack and that included myself. I've punched so many doors and walls. Luckily, the only thing I broke was the skin on my knuckles.

My temper became shorter and shorter and I realize now that it was less anger and more rage that I was trying to bury down. I hated where I was in my life. I loved the people that were in my life but I just hated myself and never felt like I measured up.

# 5 TEA FOR THE TILLERMAN

Seagulls sing your hearts away

'Cause while the sinners sin, the children play

Oh Lord, how they play and play

For that happy day, for that happy day

-Cat Stevens

Somehow, in the fall of 2009, I got a job as an elementary school teacher. This was one of the best things that ever happened to me. Whenever I finished my online classes to become a teacher, I applied for teaching jobs all across the state which is really saying something in Texas. People ask me all the time how I ended up in East Texas and the answer is simple. They were literally the only ones that even wanted to interview me. I learned a lot about myself while I tried to not end up on the news for murdering the 22 kids I was responsible for.

The first thing I learned from teaching is that I could never be God. I think it was the second Monday of my first year that I thought about bringing a water hose to class and flooding the room and locking the doors behind me. Teaching is like being a farmer that knows there's a storm coming. You can prepare all you want but you're probably gonna lose a chicken or two by the end of the day. I never lost a kid but I did like to joke about accidentally leaving them on field trips. My principal didn't enjoy that joke near as much as I did.

Those kids taught me a lot about myself. If I had been honest with myself I would have seen that some of my outburst were way too quick and way too harsh. I can't tell you how many times I went off on those poor kids.

My first year was hell. Pure and simple. I'm sure this was for a myriad of reasons but I think it boils down to two reasons. One, I was an inexperienced teacher that let the kids get too crazy before trying to calm them back down. Second, each one of those kids was possessed by Beelzebub himself. True story. Just for general information, administration likes to have a heads up when you schedule an exorcism.

I had the sweetest little girl, though, my first year, that had a crush on me. It was funny because she would tell everyone she met that we were buying land out in the country to start a farm of some sort. This was when I realized how ingrained it is for women to like people that are mean to them because that poor girl required a lot of redirecting.

I also had a little boy my first year that had a really bad temper and may end up finding out that he's bipolar himself. His whole demeanor would change out of nowhere. He hit me in the face with a paper once and I don't know what my face did but it apparently let him know that wasn't cool. He really ended up being one of my favorite people in the world. Not just kids. I hope I run into him again sometime.

The sad thing about being a teacher, especially a male teacher, is that people think there's a chance that you may be a creeper. No matter what I do to protect myself, all it would take is one child making up some kind of story and almost the entire world would be against me. That always scared me about being a teacher and it makes very little sense since just as many women are guilty of that horrible decision. Anyway, it is what it is and no one wants to feel sorry for white men. Racists.

One thing I learned from teaching was the destructive power of negativity. It is insane how one person, or kid, can totally kill the momentum of anything just by being a stick in the mud or shooting down everything you say. I really took this lesson to heart for awhile but my negativity became so systemic that I couldn't really even recognize how negative I had become.

The rage that drove me was honed while I was a teacher. The fact that I never had a panic attack while teaching is kind of surprising because it was just as stressful as any other aspect of my life. Like I've said, a lot of my anxiety was more from suppressed rage that I couldn't express. The kids definitely fell into this category.

The second year went much, much smoother. I can still remember the first day of the second year when I was trying to be a hard ass and at the last second I got a new student. This little girl was the cutest, sweetest little girl that God has ever made. The only downside, from a teaching perspective, was that she spoke exactly zero English. I was technically the ESL teacher but all that meant was I took a test that I guessed through. I was woefully unprepared. Luckily I lived in Mexico for a semester at Texas Tech when I realized my advisor had forgotten that I needed sixteen hours of a foreign language and I wanted to graduate in six months.

On that first day, I was doing my whole schtick about being Billy Badass when I realized that no matter what horrible thing I said in whatever horrible tone that sweet, sweet little girl would just smile at me and nod her head as if to say "you're right, Senor Burt." Billy Badass was broken that day. I would get mad and want to climb up to the roof to jump off and then I'd remember that little blessing God gave me and search through the room for that supportive smile.

She ended up going back to Mexico at the end of the year and I always wonder how she's doing. That goes for all of my students. The problem about being a single male teacher that wants to see the kids he became so attached to is that if I call and ask them to hang out I end up with a special new ID.

I had a few students that were ADHD and it was so sad to see them try and keep their attention and just not be able to. Sad and annoying but mostly sad. I had one student that could never really figure out his medicine and was always just a hot mess. Broke my heart. There were days he would just sit and cry.

I also had a bad boy in my class that I couldn't stand for about the first two or three weeks because he was just so awful and mean to everyone. Then one day I saw him reading a book in the back of the room about a puppy and cheesing out big time. From that moment on I loved that kid. He had gotten in trouble each year and kicked out of his classes but I was the only one that was able to keep him in the room all year.

His problem was just that school didn't interest him and, lets be honest, school isn't that interesting when you've grown up in the information age that these kids have. The way I got through to him, though, was letting whoever made the best grades on their six weeks test write on my face with permanent marker and I had to keep it on all day. I have never seen anyone work so diligently and so in tune with every detail. I knew instantly that he took the bait and luckily he didn't end up drawing a penis on my face.

I had a lot of supportive friends that were teachers there that made me surviving those few years possible. If it wasn't for my great principal, smiling first grade teachers, and the Hutchinson family I wouldn't have made it.

That being said, some teachers are awful. It killed me when teachers would put their own stresses above the stresses that the kids had. I taught in Crockett, Texas, and it was a very poor socioeconomic environment. There is something infuriating about a middle aged Christian woman crying because she doesn't know how she is going to teach math to a girl that just had a miscarriage in the fourth grade. Seriously. Who cares about math at that point? At that point, you just need to be a human and care for the kid. Long division is pointless now and the kids know it. Just use a calculator and be a support to the kids.

Everyone always asks me why I quit teaching. They always laugh when I say I only did it for two years because they think I either hated it or didn't like kids. Both of these reasons are dead wrong. The problem was me.

You have to be healthy to be able to help other people. I was already broken but I just didn't know it. I was alone on the opposite side of Texas. My weekends were either spent watching mindless TV or drinking by myself because I couldn't understand why my mind wouldn't slow down. I want to make sure its clear that I rarely drank just for the enjoyment but more often than not it was just so I could have some peace from myself.

My negativity was already in full swing and I couldn't see any way I could really have a successful life by following the rules and staying a teacher. Insanely more than this, I felt like I had been lied to my entire life. Good, responsible choices rarely lead you to something good. The reward is supposed to be being a good person and, in the time of Facebook, that doesn't measure up to what all your friends are doing. You can't take a picture to show that 'oh hey, I don't have a boat but I help people everyday'.

The key to me that drove me to quit teaching was that I couldn't in good conscience spread that lie to those poor kids that honestly have a hard life ahead of them. They are low socioeconomic kids that were mostly African American in a small town that had zero industry unless you count meth. For the most part, those kids will have to do amazing in school just to get the same chances that I squandered and didn't deserve but got because of my skin tone.

This also made me think that, with those chances, I needed to do something bigger. I owed it to the kids to be a better person. My intent when I quit teaching was to move back to Sweetwater and help my mom, go to nursing school and become a nurse anesthetist, and just be an all-around badass. Only one of those things actually happened. I'm an LVN that has zero interest in being an RN.

# 6 OH MY SWEET CAROLINA

Oh my sweet Carolina

What compels me to go?

Oh my sweet disposition

May you one day carry me home

-Ryan Adams

Like many people who move back to their hometowns, I felt out of place in the very town I had always wanted to live in. Your hometown is never really what you remember it being and a lot of the time it just serves to remind you how much everything has changed. I found myself constantly comparing myself to that change and could never really find my place. The majority of my friends had moved away and the others were understandably busy with familial obligations.

After nursing school, I expected there to be tons of jobs available for new nurses. Unfortunately, there weren't many employers that wanted nurses that had zero experience. I don't really blame them. I graduated knowing nothing about being a nurse or helping people. All I knew was how to pick out the right answers on a test.

I worked at a nursing home, the place where dreams go to die, for a few days until I was told that the Director of Nursing had lied to me about them offering insurance. My money was running low and I had already quit working at the same grocery store I had years earlier. We had clinical days at the state school during nursing school but I hated every single day of it. Unfortunately, they paid more than anywhere else in town so I applied and got the job quickly.

After I got through the month-long training period I started on home number 5972. 5972 was full of developmentally disabled individuals that for the most part couldn't walk or talk. About seven of them suffered from seizures so to say that it was an exhausting environment would be underselling the daily stress that I got used to.

Even with their limited knowledge of me, there wasn't a single coworker that didn't tell me that I needed to take better care of myself or find a woman for that position. I just laughed it off and discounted it. I knew I was pushing myself but didn't realize how hard I was being or the toll it was taking. I would generally work about sixty hours a week most of the time. The most I ever worked was eighty-four hours in a week from working doubles. I was trying to pay off debt and move into a different bracket of living.

The only problem is that none of them had known me long enough to know how truly unhappy I was. In their defense, I didn't know either. The guy they knew was funny and usually smiling but secretly dying on the inside. He would get mad and go off on people in a flash. I would always apologize but it usually took twenty-four hours for me to realize just how large of a tool I was being.

I worked there on and off for two years and I miss the guys I took care of every single day. I made a lot of good friends while I worked there. The staff that directly took care of the guys were some of the best people I've ever known. The majority were people that I probably never would have met had I not worked there. One of the best lessons I learned while I was there was how honest and real each of them were even if it was messy. Granted, the realness got old sometimes but it was in stark opposition of how I was acting.

While I was in nursing school, I took a vacation by myself down to Key West and had a great time. The best part, by far, was going skydiving over the ocean. I had always wanted to but I was deathly scared of heights. When it came time to jump I made a decision in my head to push the fear and stress to the back of my mind and just do it. I stepped out into the now open doorway and did my best to not vomit all over myself.

Going skydiving is one of my favorite decisions I've made but I think my mindset of pushing everything down and going through the motions lasted from then until I had a moment of clarity at rock bottom. I took all of the stress from work and buried it down until I was about to blow. From this point on I was different levels of manic but I had no idea.

When I would get to a point in my life where I couldn't handle my head spinning anymore, I would usually abuse alcohol and try to have an exciting night to release some of the energy. It worked for a while but, obviously, at some point it was just too much. I became an openly angry person that had no problem going off on people.

On top of work, I was working out six days a week and barely eating. For whatever reason, I wanted to be as skinny as possible and then really bulk up. Three years of doing that later, I am still trying to be skinnier which meant on top of work, I was barely eating or drinking because I didn't want to go up a tenth of a pound the next day.

I was also taking two classes at Cisco Junior College to try and continue my nursing career. I was taking Microbiology and Nutrition which is oddly an in depth class. I had taken Micro years earlier when I met Shea but dropped it because I was going to have to "read" and "learn new things".

The most exhausting thing I was doing, though, was trying to keep up the illusion that I was the same person I had always been. That was work's one saving grace because I didn't have to pretend to be happy. I went from being a very out-going, caring person that would do anything for anyone to this person that would wear headphones without music playing so people would leave him alone. I used sarcasm and inflection to hide how little I cared about generally everything and everyone. Including myself. I would say horrible things about myself in my mind. I would yell at myself in mirrors at home and at work I would either mouth the words in the mirror or just give myself the finger.

It all started slowly. The first time you give yourself the finger in the mirror its kind of funny. It gets less so when it includes yelling and you're waving both fingers in your own face like a crazy person.

The only way I was able to keep all this up and still have

enough energy was pumping my body full of caffeine. On any given day I would have at least a cup of coffee, three energy drinks, and preworkout that is basically an energy drink with creatine. I would basically not eat anything which basically threw me into a fight or flight mindset every single day at one of the most stressful homes at one of the most stressful nursing jobs in town. What I thought was fight or flight would end up being something else. Something way, way worse. On the flip side of that, I would randomly abuse alcohol just to be able to deal with what all I was my putting my body through.

Sometime during the winter semester at Cisco, I started having panic attacks again. I would start to hyperventilate, cry, and generally believe that the decisions I had made with my life had pushed me into a corner that was closing in on me and was going to kill me. I told no one but did have to drop my classes.

This went on and got worse over the next six months. I would have to leave the gym, hide at work, and cancel plans so I could have panic attacks in secret. I honestly just thought I needed to toughen up and carry on which I did until the end of summer.

On whichever Saturday it ended up being, I had panic attacks the entire day but hid them by staying in the med room at work whenever possible. I would have my panic attack, clean up my face, take a deep breath, and then go pass meds. As soon as I got done I went back into the med room and repeated that once more before I left the state school for the last time. I decided that night that I had to change something if I was gonna make it.

Unfortunately, that choice was not to go to a treatment center. I chose to fall back on my heredity and move across the country leaving everyone that I cared about behind. It was the single most self-destructive, paralyzing thing I've ever done. To date, I don't regret any mistake more than this one. Leaving behind people who cared about me at a time when I needed that was the dumbest thing I could do. Part of me knew something was really wrong with me and I didn't want to continue hurting people I care about. On a less selfless side, I also didn't want to seem weak in front of people.

I went to South Carolina to live with my brother and his wife who are the greatest people in the world. While I was there, though, the lack of my usual routine and the amazing friends I left behind showed just how sick I was.

Over the next two months, I had at least 100 panic attacks. I finally started to tell people that something was wrong and went to the doctor who gave me Paxil and Ativan. The Ativan definitely helped but the Paxil just slowed my mind down enough to concentrate on the worst aspects of my life. A few days in, it made me have suicidal thoughts for the first time in my life. Those thoughts are gone now but just having them at all scars you.

I had gotten the pills from going to a urgent care doctor and that was a huge mistake. If you are going to take antipsychotics you truly need to go to a psychologist. The pills can mess with you so badly that you need to be under a watchful eye as you get used to your meds. Taking the easy way out almost killed me.

The Paxil and continued panic attacks finally drove me back to Abilene to get help but just barely. Just like the drive to South Carolina, the drive home was filled with panic attacks the whole way. On the way back, I had to stop and get a hotel so I could rest.  Sadly, I woke up at three in the morning having a panic attack.  I had to pace back and forth across the room for two hours before I could fall back asleep.

When I got back home I was basically having constant panic attacks that would start as soon as I woke up (if I was lucky enough to not wake up in one) and I could no longer even think and I finally looked physically like I had felt mentally for years.  I had to lean on any friend I've ever had that called my contact list on my phone home.

I just wanted to give up.  I didn't want to die but I just had nothing left.  My fight was gone.  Finally, I said out loud that I wanted to give up and I realized that I needed to get actual help.

# 7 SOMETHING PRETTY

I was a dumb punk kid with nothing to lose

And too much weight for walking shoes.

I could have died from being boring.

As for loneliness,

She greets me every morning.

-Patrick Park

Entering a treatment center was the hardest and easiest decision I've ever had to make. I knew I needed help but it also acknowledged the fact that I was at rock bottom. I was running out of money and running friendships too thin asking for advice that I would ultimately ignore. The day that I finally decided to go came after having way too much to drink with friends back in Abilene.

I've always been a sporadic drinker at best but when I do drink it's a lot. My drinking would be like a crutch if you only had to use it when the weather got cold. I had the best time with my friends that night and I remember thinking that all my problems were gone and I could just be myself. That moment of clarity was definitely gone the next morning when I woke up on a friend's couch.

That feeling of ease was replaced with one of dread when I realized that voice in my head was back and he was not amused. I woke up before my friends and walked about two miles back to my car, if not further just because I was so anxious I couldn't sit still.

I finally made it back to my car and sat there for a second gathering myself. This was proven even harder when I remembered that I had broken my glasses in half on purpose in what can only be termed a 'feat of strength'. Apparently rum and coke is a homeopathic cure for farsightedness. The more you know! It's important to keep in mind that for the next month or so I was walking and driving around blind without my glasses.

I made the drive back over to Sweetwater, having panic attacks the majority of the way, and called my aunt to see if I could talk to her. We discussed, just as I had with my mom and brother, treatment centers and decided on Carrollton Springs near Dallas. It was really less discussing and more me saying I needed to go and crying like I had just seen the beginning of the movie Up for the first time.

This decision came after about a month of thinking how much I just wanted to give up. Like I said before, I didn't want to die and especially not in a way that would traumatize others, but I just had no fight left in me. Even lifting my head off the pillow first thing in the morning was a struggle. On this day, though, I actually said it out loud and that scared me.

The main reasons I finally decided to get help was the fear that I would become a full blown alcoholic because I had felt so amazing. I was also afraid that there may not be much time between saying you want to give up and literally giving up. Also, on a drastically happier note, I have a niece on the way and I did not want to be like this when she got here.

So with those things in mind I gave up control and my mom, my aunt, and myself headed to Dallas. I barely slept the night before. I was worried about what was really gonna end up being wrong with me but I knew I couldn't ignore it anymore. At this point, I would just start crying for no apparent reason to the outside world. In my head, the reason was clear. I couldn't stop thinking about the people I had hurt and the fear that I would never stop hurting people.

I texted just about everyone in my phone to let them know what was happening. Everyone was, of course, supportive. My last meal on the outside was an animal style double-double from In and Out with well done fries. I recommend trying it; the burger not mental breakdown.

When I got to the treatment center, they interviewed me to see what they thought may be wrong and make sure I wasn't on drugs. After that I had to tell my family bye and give over all of my control to these people in hopes of getting better. In this case, giving up control meant giving up a lot of freedoms. I had to give them my cell phone (I was devastated), my shoelaces were replaced with zip ties so I didn't hang myself, and the most disconcerting became aware as I walked through three sets of doors that all locked behind me. Locks that I didn't have the keys to. From this point on, I will stop saying treatment center and now refer to it as either the nut house or the looney bin. There's no political correctness on the inside.

As I realized that I had just agreed voluntarily to imprison myself I met some of the people that I was gonna be living with for hopefully just a week. My mind was just about gone simply from exhaustion via the panic attack smorgasbord my life had become. I was also busy trying to figure out the living situation I had just stepped into.

There were three different units and I got lucky to get on the nice one. For the most part everyone on my end of the nut house were there for mental health issues like mine. The other two units were set up more for chemical dependency. Not to say we didn't have anyone fighting addiction.

I met my roommate who was a nice, quiet Vietnamese

guy about my age. As far as roommates in the looney bin go, I got really lucky. He may not have with me but who knows. My psychiatrist had already left for the day so my first day was spent getting settled and meeting everyone. It was amazing how easy it is to get to know people when you have your guard down. There's no reason to act like something you're not when you've all gone to crazy town. Unless, I suppose, you have multiple personalities and some definitely did.

The following day I finally saw my psychiatrist and I really lucked out. He looked exactly like the Math teacher that Kevin Arnold had in Wonder Years, Mr. Collins. I knew how much I lucked out when I saw that one of the other doctors looked like one of the bad guys from Indiana Jones and the Temple of Doom.

My initial diagnosis was severe anxiety and depression. They put me on the max dose of Zoloft and started me on a ton of Ativan. When I worked at the state school we would give 2 mg for really, really bad seizures. Over the course of those next three days, I got 13 mg. and that was on top of my max dose of Zoloft. I was as calm as a Hindu cow.

I know the 13 mg seems like a huge, dangerous dose but it finally got me back to a normal level. I really don't know the last time I was at a normal level. Probably that day five or so years earlier when I got back from WalMart to hear that my life had been turned upside down. I was coherent throughout (as far as I know at least) and could for the first time feel myself creeping up into anxiety or down to depression before it was out of control. Before I was basically a prisoner to whatever emotion my body chose to have. Not to say that I was not responsible for anything I said or did because I definitely am.

The week that I spent in the looney bin was the hardest, best week of my life. It was horribly depressing and literally insanely funny at the very same time. I met some people that were my kind of crazy and we would sit wide-eyed as we, crazy/drugged, watched other crazy/drugged people. We were all on sensory overload the whole time.

When I did get out, my diagnosis hadn't changed but my

mindset definitely had. I spent an entire week with a lot of people that the majority of the world had given up on and realized that I was no better. There was a homeless lesbian heroin addict there that I grew to admire so deeply. It was amazing to watch someone fight so hard. Anytime I want to give up now I think of her.

I cannot tell you what it's like to be free outside after being pinned up for an entire week. I felt like Morgan Freeman near the end of Shawshank. It was beautiful but moved so damn quick. The week on the inside was strictly regimented and the excessive stimulation made my mind just about as mushy as it had been in the first place. My hands shook almost as bad as my voice quivered for about three days.

As soon as I got home I put up a status on Facebook apologizing for the way I had been acting and started this new transparent way of living. I can't tell you how much all the love and support means to me. I wish I could go back and tell the guy that was hiding all of his problems that there was no reason. If anyone reading this is hiding stuff like that, or different stuff, please don't wait as long as I did.

That's the main reason I've decided to be so open about something that most people would understandably hide. Aside from it being therapeutic to get all this out, I would see it as a great failing if I went through all of that on my own when I didn't need to only to allow someone else to make my own mistakes. "Smart people learn from their mistakes. But the real sharp ones learn from the mistakes of others." That quote is from Brandon Mull. I found it online and have no idea who he is. If he's a serial killer you should probably take his advice with a grain of salt.

If it hadn't been for my super honest Facebook status, I may have never realized what was actually wrong with me. When I got out of the treatment center I was still diagnosed with severe anxiety and depression. Sadly that was just the tip of the iceberg. The medicine definitely helped make me happier but I was still having random panic attacks and was still just very down.

If realizing I needed to go get help was rock bottom I found myself still at rock bottom but at least standing up trying to figure out a way to claw my way back up.

# 8 TIME ALONE

Time, they say, can heal you

Though, that's harder to believe

When you meet the broken hearted

And see what it meant to leave

-Joshua Hyslop

The last day in the nut house was bittersweet because I knew I was going to have to come back out to a world that had total kicked my butt and I had to decide how I was gonna handle everything. A large part of me wanted to just hide and stay in the house forever but I had promised myself before I went in that I was gonna be totally upfront about everything.

I took a week off between the looney bin and going to talk

to my therapist. My hands and voice shook for three days straight from all the stress both building up to and being in the nuthouse. I didn't sleep for two and a half days. I would just lay in bed trying to comprehend what I had just been through. I couldn't even begin to remember all the crazy stuff I saw that week. We all joked on the inside that we had probably developed PTSD from the whole experience but we had no idea where we should go to fix that.

I talked to very few people for that entire week. I went into Abilene and drove around some. Of course, I drove to all the most depressing places I could think of because I grew up watching Dawson's Creek and it felt natural. Luckily, I at least held off on the 'in the arms of an angel' song. A close friend of mine told me that it was like I was trying my best to be depressed on purpose. This was when I realized how much work I had to do because you can take all the pills you want but they can't make you choose to be happy.

I had been unhappy for so long that I had developed all these self-defeating, self-deprecating ways of living. One of my best friends had to constantly remind me to always be aware of your thoughts and ask yourself if they are positive and constructive or negative and destructive and that was some of the best advice I've ever had.   I had a panic attack the day that I drove around. One of the worst I've ever had.

I spent the rest of the week down that I had another panic attack that I just basically slept and nodded at people that came across my path.  I would text people but I had zero interest in talking.  I really had zero interest in anything.  My main thought was just how much work it was going to be to rebuild my life and missing the life that I had before I blew it up on the way out of town to South Carolina.

When I went to the therapist that Monday he was confused about where all I had been, which is something I've gotten used to explaining over the years.  I told him about the treatment center and how I asked the psychiatrist to Goodwill Hunting me and keep telling me 'its not your fault'. The psych laughed but, in the end, refused.

It took all of about five seconds for my therapist to say he thought I may be bipolar. From the little bit I knew about it at the time, I was afraid he was right. Two days later I was able to get into another psychiatrist in Dallas and those fears were confirmed.

I am Bipolar 1 with severe agitation. The severe agitation is what caused the panic attacks that I was going through. Unfortunately, Bipolar 1 with severe agitation has a thirty six times higher chance of committing suicide.

That's when I knew just how seriously I was going to have to take everything. Everyone in my family and my inner circle were shocked to find out that I was bipolar because the idea of the disorder has been overblown into a caricature of someone screaming only to start crying soon after. Real talk, I've done this so the caricature fits at times but that was before meds.

Everything that I had apologized for on Facebook were signs and symptoms of what I apparently had. The scary thing, to me, is that I'm the type of bipolar that runs the risk of falling into psychoses. It is incredibly clear from the start that I was going to have to be insanely vigilant on taking pills and watching my moods. It may be weird but I was instantly thankful for the hell that I had just been through because if it had been even a shade easier I wouldn't take it as seriously as it needs to be.

Bipolar disorder is starting to be seen more as a physiological problem than mental which is great in my eyes. The basics of bipolar disorder is extremely similar to how diabetes affects the body. Instead of your pancreas and insulin your brain and dopamine are the problem. My brain basically never gives me the right amount of dopamine to react to a problem so I overreact more often than not.

Its called bipolar, though, because you switch back and forth between two extremes. The extreme high is called mania and the low is called manic depression. When you're high you feel great (don't tell my future kids that I said that). If you're manic your mind thinks six times faster than normal and you come up with all these really great ideas but there's no logic behind them. Your mind gets so jacked up that your prefrontal cortex, basically considered where your conscience lives, shuts off.

The bad thing about this is that as soon as it happens, you lose all ability to have foresight, insight, or have any empathy. The real hell of it is that when you get as bad as I was, it shuts off completely for six to eight weeks. Weeks. It takes around one hundred days for your brain to actually start functioning again normally and I believe that. When we left the treatment center I couldn't even read a map or hold a conversation. I would lose my thought mid-sentence over and over.

Another mixed blessing is when you're in a mixed state. This is what happened to me when I ran away from my problems to South Carolina. To sum up, the whole time that I was using energy drinks and all that caffeine I was in a manic state and I couldn't function outside of it. My abuse of alcohol was me self medicating trying to fix a problem I didn't realize I was actually having. The second I left a friends' house in Abilene telling them bye I went from being high as a kite (still don't tell the kids) to falling about one hundred miles into a slab of concrete. I literally had panic attacks the whole way to South Carolina and just kept saying over and over "what are you doing?" with and without expletives. This left me in a mixed state where I was intensely depressed but my mind was still flying at six times the normal speed on the most depressing things I could imagine. The part that scares me the most is the fear of becoming manic again and my prefrontal cortex shutting off and blowing up my life all over again.

Finding out that I was bipolar while I was unemployed was great because it's a full time job changing behaviors and figuring out a new routine that makes room for your new problem. I will always be bipolar. There's no cure. There is medicine that will help keep me on an even level but I still have to be hypervigilant on noticing any small swings one way or the other. Basically my entire life style that I was living is the exact opposite of what you are supposed to do.

You aren't supposed to have a stressful job. Of course, every job is stressful so it's a matter of finding one that has stress levels I can handle. You're supposed to never work overtime, or swing shifts. You're supposed to get eight to twelve hours of sleep a night. No caffeine or alcohol is preferred.

It doesn't scare me that I will have to deal with this every day of my life, it scares me that perhaps at one point I won't take it seriously and I'll backslide. This is when I'll need a support system and I've been so blessed by everyone lately to the point that I know I'll always have someone I can call.

The hardest part is realizing that there are some things that I broke while I was sick that I will probably never get back. I just have to keep my eyes on God and know that he will fix the things that need fixing and I just need to trust in Him. That and take my medicine.

That is one pet peeve I have and I used to be guilty of it. I couldn't understand how someone couldn't just pick themselves up when they were sad and just get over stuff. That all changed when no matter what I did I couldn't get myself to be positive or do anything to better myself. The thought, though, that a lot of people in churches go without treatment or hide their problems because of the concern others will think that it means something is wrong with their walk with God.

# 9 ORANGE SKY

Well I had a dream

I stood beneath an orange sky

With my brother and my sister standing by

-Alexi Murdoch

Over the next couple weeks, I slowly processed my week in the nut house. When I was at my lowest, most stressed out moment I had a moment of blinding clarity. It came while I was at the nuthouse this last summer. I was sitting right next to Yoga Pants, the amazing friend I made in that crazy place.

She was on my right side the majority of the week. To

my other side was the most psychotic, exhausting person I've ever met. We will call him Billy because he reminded me of the character Billy Madison before he went to school and saw the error in his ways. Standing in front of him was the crazy lady who thought she was God. They were both laughing maniacally, staring at me for some sort of affirmation. While I was repressing this memory, I looked over at Yoga Pants who had the same look of overload flooding her face.

It was Sunday and my last full day on the inside. It was the longest day for all of us. My Jordanian friend was overdosed, by choice, on sleeping pills and slept the entire day. Yoga Pants and I had become friends with Billy a few days earlier. When he showed up he was just in a hospital gown and it took all day for either of us to be able to comprehend this fact because our minds were so exhausted.

I finally asked him why and he said that he didn't have a shirt and that he didn't deserve one. Without thinking I got up and went into my room and got him a shirt like another friend had done for me earlier in the week.

By the look on his face, this was the nicest thing anyone had ever done for him. Twenty four hours later I realized I had met my own version of Zach Galifinakis in Due Date. Billy was paranoid schizophrenic and also very hungry for attention. Yoga Pants and I spent our first two days with him buying his schtick and feeling really bad for the guy. On Sunday, we both realized that a lot of it was for attention and we just couldn't handle the show anymore.

That's not to say that his need for attention was any less tragic. I ran out of patience with him but I don't know what could have happened to him to make him think he had to act such a way to keep friends. We would have been more than happy to get to know the real person behind the act.

According to him, he was admitted for having a bad reaction to some rosemary he shot into his vein. Rosemary isn't some new drug you need to be worried about. It's the rosemary that is in your kitchen cupboard and is not a drug. I thought he was homeless until family night when I saw that his parents looked remarkably normal and exhausted by their son.

It's funny how even on the inside you find yourself taking solace in being less crazy than others. Am I really any less crazy than him? Probably not. We are just different kinds of crazy. What was scary about Billy and Crazy Lady was that I could see the logic in their delusion. That's a scary thing when the crazies start to make sense to you.

I think that's why I lost any kind feelings toward him because it scared me that I could, at some point, be in that bad of shape. Being bipolar, there's always a chance that I could fall into psychosis where I act and believe like they did. That's why I take my disorder so seriously. I don't want to put myself or my loved ones through something like that.

Anyway, moment of clarity: while they were looking to me for affirmation, my mind just had enough. I had been on sensory overload for an entire week and trying to take Billy seriously pushed me over the edge. With my mind numbed, I forced my eyes shut harder than I ever have and the darkness you usually see wasn't there.

I think, in that moment, my mind retreated to and recognized a happy, safe place to stay. When I closed my eyes I could feel the sun glaring in my face and I could barely make out the rest of what my mind was trying to show me. Behind the glare was an orange sky and I was rocking back and forth on a sailboat on a lake or the ocean. The colors were so vibrant and I could feel the sun on my skin as if I was outside and not locked inside with Yoga Pants and the clinically insane.

I still think about that moment and like to imagine it more in depth each time. I can feel the spray of the water coming up over the side of the boat and can see the sun changing between different colors of orange and pink. I don't presently know how to sail but I do want to learn at some point in my life and make this moment a reality. I don't know what Heaven will be like but for me this would be plenty. The only thing I would add to my happy place is someone to enjoy it with.

That's one thing I learned from going to South Carolina. I was in one of the most beautiful places I've ever been and all I wanted was someone to share it with. It reminds me of the movie

"Into the Wild". At the end he realized that for happiness to be real it has to be shared. I could have been so happy in South Carolina but my heart was empty and alone. I spent most of my time going to the lake floating in the water up to my shoulders looking back to the shore wishing there was a woman looking up from her book smiling at me, or even better, floating right next to me.

Back in reality, Yoga Pants was going to see her family at visitation and it was one of the few nights I didn't have any visitors so I went into my room and laid on my bed trying to hold onto the vision I had just had. It was when I was laying there in the dark imagining riding on those waves that everything snapped into place.

This was when I realized how prideful I had been and just how much I had used anger to drive myself. I realized that everyone in the nut house was just doing their best with the cards they were dealt and I slowly let that grace flow to people I knew on the outside. It's so easy to blame others for our problems but no one is really to blame for any of my problems. No one has ever set out to hurt me and even if they have it had more to do with them than with me.

Almost 99 percent of the world, I think, is out there trying their best to make sense of the world they find themselves in. My world isn't your world and vice versa. We are all just passing by eachother as little blips on eachother's horizons as we play out our own view of how life works. We are all told what to believe by people that came before us and none of us were told the exact same things.

I always thought I wanted to have kids but I'm not really sure that I'm ready for that type of responsibility. I know I could mindlessly raise a kid like anyone else but being aware of the power and presence you have over someone else's life isn't something to take lightly. No matter what I do, I will miss something as far as parenting goes and affect their lives in one way or another. Even a perfect parent, if they existed, still has to send their kid off into an imperfect world.

For me, for now, I'm just headed towards that orange sky.

I just hope when I get there I'm not alone.

# 10 WINDOWS ARE ROLLED DOWN

Corn rows have companion feel

This rocky road and this steering wheel

Who do you call to ease your pain

I hope for you to get through this rain


Roughly four years have passed since I sat down to write "Bipolar Express". When I wrote it, I was freshly diagnosed as Bipolar 1 with severe agitation. With this came a sense of relief just to know what was wrong with me. That came across, in my writing, through humor and sarcasm.

As I sit here today, I'm much more somber. I have only had one panic attack since I wrote this book. I've had a few close calls but nothing too serious. I'm somber, though, because this road that I'm on is a tiring one. It is also one that I constantly feel like the world wants me to take in silence.

Since I wrote this book, very much has changed. I spent a year in Corpus Christi, Texas, working as a nurse. I really enjoyed my time there but it was a lot of hard work that was really trying for my anxiety. I didn't realize it at the time but I was taking too many Ativan to deal with it. I no longer take Ativan because I don't like the way it brushes your mind clean of all recent memory.

I'm no longer a nurse. I have gone back to teaching and really enjoy my students. Just as they did before, the kids in my classroom teach me so much about myself and life itself. I have been blessed this year with possibly the sweetest group of kids ever assembled.

Over the years, I have gotten quieter about my diagnosis but I still share it with those closest to me. It wears on me that I have this diagnosis that has such a stigma. Part of me wants to forget that it exists and not ever tell another person. I'm medicated now and show very little signs of the disorder on a daily basis.

I love my kids, in my class, so dearly that it keeps me honest on how I am treating them. While I do have to raise my voice from time to time, I make it a point to provide a positive environment for them to grow in. Like I said, I am beyond blessed by the kids that I'm responsible for.

If I have any problems now, it is mainly anxiety. I feel anxiety at every turn and it wears me down. I miss more family get togethers than I would like to admit and steer clear of most social situations that I find myself in. Luckily, I have been blessed with a great group of coworkers that I know would do anything for me.

I still find happiness along the highway. I drive with my windows rolled down and the radio up whenever possible. I'm at peace with who I am right now. If there's one caveat to that, though, it's that I think I need to be more vocal about mental health. That is probably what led me back to the keyboard on this topic.

We all have mental health issues. Some are just more acceptable than others. I don't know what a world where I'm totally upfront about my life will look like but I know I need to head that direction even if that means a lot of big changes. All I know is I care deeply for all of those around me and I am so thankful for the space they give me to be imperfect.

On one last side note, I sincerely apologize for the lack of ending this book once had. I was still not in a good place when I plastered this book together four years ago but now I'm healthy and clear and wanted to fix this book that stands to date as the most honest 'story' I will ever be able to tell.

## ABOUT THE AUTHOR

Gabriel Cougar Burt is just another man trying to make sense of the life he's been given.

www.ingramcontent.com/pod-product-compliance
Lightning Source LLC
Chambersburg PA
CBHW070755290526
45795CB00002B/564